EMBRACING THE MYSTERY
LIVING THE LIFE YOU WANT

ACKNOWLEDGEMENTS

With special thanks to Carol Moore, Linda Reeves,
and Jill Shewburg, for taking time to proof-read my manuscript.

DEDICATION

To my wife Carol and our family of Kevin, Chris, Paul and Beth for their love, friendship, and humour.

To my Mother and Father who not only gave me the precious gift of life but also an insatiable sense of wonder and curiosity.

To my friends who generously give me space and distance without judgment.

To my sister, Pat, who introduced me to the computer.

To Harriett - a friend forever.

EMBRACING THE MYSTERY
LIVING THE LIFE YOU WANT

MIKE MOORE

Artwork: Mike Moore
Cover photo by: Larry McNally, Haviland Bay, Lake Superior

Library and Archives Canada Cataloguing in Publication

Moore, Mike, 1942-
   Embracing the mystery : living the life you want / Mike Moore. -- Revised ed.

ISBN 978-0-9685029-0-7

   1. Self-actualization (Psychology). 2. Moore, Mike, 1942- --Anecdotes. I. Title.

BF637.S4M6654 2011   158.1   C2011-904009-3

Motivational Plus Publishing
Brantford, Ontario, Canada.
Copyright © Mike Moore 1998

Printed by Ball Media
ballmedia.com
4th Printing

ISBN 0-9685029-0-7

CONTENTS

INTRODUCTION i

HUMOUR/THE MIND/BODY CONNECTION 2
STRESS AND PEACE OF MIND 11
ATTITUDE IS EVERYTHING 25
SELF ESTEEM 39
SELF TALK 43
FEAR 48
WELLNESS 53
FRIENDSHIP 60
MALE BONDING 61
PATIENCE 62
PIZZAZZ 65
LANGUAGE AND REALITY 66
ENLIGHTENED MALADJUSTMENT 67
AGING AND DEATH 68
SUMMER OF SADNESS 73
PARENTING/FAMILY 74
HEALING THE EARTH 81
WISDOM AND NATURE 83
RANDOM REFLECTIONS 86
JUST FOR THE FUN OF IT 91

INTRODUCTION

When you write a book about effective living there is a real danger of your readers thinking that you have mastered the art. Let me assure you from the start that nothing could be farther from the truth. I like to think that we are all on the road to fulfilment, each seeking to become what she/he is capable of becoming and it is a life-long process.

On many occasions people in my audiences have asked me whether I intended to write a book containing some of the material used in my talks. Like many of you I had the intention, but not the drive to make it become reality. Until now.

I believe that life is a mystery to be lived and enjoyed to the fullest, not a problem to be solved and endured. We all know that living involves pain and suffering, but we also know that pain and suffering can often be overcome, permitting the sun to shine again. This is what I sought to present within these pages, the belief in the wonder and mystery of life and the confidence to believe that we can achieve for ourselves whatever we conceive.

I do hope you enjoy the wit and the wisdom, and that you find them helpful in your own struggle to embrace the mystery of it all.

Mike Moore
Sept. 1998

March 2011 Revised Edition

"The Principle business of Life is to enjoy it!"
— Sam Butler

HUMOUR AND THE MIND / BODY CONNECTION

Ever since I was introduced to the writings of Norman Cousins in, "Anatomy of an Illness", I have been fascinated by the role of the human mind in healing and wellness, specifically the role of humour. When Norman Cousins was diagnosed with a terminal illness in midlife, he immediately set out to alter his fate.

Through attitudinal transformation he shifted his thinking from negative to positive, from fear to hope. By saturating his life with humour and laughter he was able, with the co-operation of modern medicine of course, to overcome his terminal illness.

When Cousins died a few years ago he was in his seventies and the illness had never returned. Recently, researchers at the Loma Linda Medical School in California validated the findings of Norman Cousins regarding the role of humour and laughter in healing and wellness. Doctor Stanley Tann has discovered that laughing frequently helps healthy people stay happy and healthy and sick people recover more rapidly.

He also found that laughter triggered physiological changes that benefit the lungs, muscles, heart, nerves, hormones and the entire immune system. Humour, it was discovered, kicked the immune system into high gear and actually prevented stress from undermining our immunity.

Humour was found to reduce stress levels by one half and significantly raise the levels of gamma interferon, an immune system hormone.

The activity of killer cells which destroy viruses and tumours was increased by twenty percent in the presence of laughter and humour.

"B" cells, which produce antibodies to combat diseases are empowered by laughter, and an immune system component called immunoglobulin increased by ten percent.

By the way, nervous and cynical laughter did not produce the same positive results.

THE MESSAGE IS CLEAR:
LAUGHTER IS, INDEED, THE BEST MEDICINE.

TO BECOME A LAFFOLOGIST...

- Watch funny television programs.

- Rent and view funny movies.

- Use a "Joke a day" calendar.

- Collect jokes and amusing experiences.

- Hang out with amusing people.

- Collect and enjoy cartoons.

- Train yourself to see the funny side of life.

HAVE YOU EVER WONDERED….

…if you can be a closet claustrophobic?

…why sheep don't shrink when it rains?

…why the word abbreviation is so long?

…if there is another word for thesaurus?

…why they sterilize the needles used in lethal injections?

…why kamikaze pilots wear helmets?

…why, if it's tourist season, hunters can't shoot them?

…how you know it's time to tune bagpipes?

…why there is an expiration date on sour cream?

…how come you never hear about gruntled employees?

…why they call it a TV set when you only get one?

Author unknown

THE VALUE OF HUMOUR

- ✓ Humour reduces stress levels. It is impossible to feel anxious and laugh at the same time.

- ✓ Laughter boosts morale, while stress erodes it.

- ✓ Keeping things in perspective boosts morale and humour helps us keep things in perspective.

- ✓ Humour helps facilitate change. Change is inevitable and people who laugh heartily and frequently tend to be more flexible and adaptable.

- ✓ Communication improves when humour is used appropriately. The timely use of humour can get a point across effectively and assists in the process of problem solving.

- ✓ Laughter and humour relieve boredom and increase creative energy.

- ✓ Humour builds confidence. When we laugh at ourselves, we are less rigid and more spontaneous. We tend to bounce back more quickly when negative things happen. Humour also makes us less fearful of making mistakes and more confident in overcoming setbacks.

- ✓ Laughter promotes positive relationships. When you hear a funny story your first impulse is to tell someone and share the laughter. When laughter is shared a natural bonding occurs.

- ✓ Humour promotes happiness and joy. It's good to be alive.

- ✓ Joy and laughter are the natural results of doing the work we love.

- ✓ *"Once you find humour in any situation, you can survive it."*
    Bill Cosby

- ✓ *"A person without a sense of humour is like a wagon without springs; it is jolted by every pebble in the road."*
    Henry Ward Beecher

- ✓ Humour gives us the power to go on.

- ✓ Laughter is like changing a baby's diaper; it doesn't get rid of the mess permanently, but it makes things OK for awhile.

- ✓ Humour cultivates a lightness of spirit in the face of life's weighty matters.

- ✓ Humour helps us thrive, not just survive.

- ✓ Quality relationships are measured by laughter. When relationships are good people laugh a lot.

✓ The humour I speak of must never be based on laughing at someone, racism, sexism, put downs, sarcasm or ridicule. These forms of humour are destructive attempts to make one look good by making another look and feel badly. There is enough good humour to last a lifetime. Just look for it.

THEY WHO LAUGH..... LAST

Laughter is the #1 Stress Buster

STRESS AND PEACE OF MIND

In my work as a motivational speaker I am frequently asked to come and make people feel good about themselves, life and their workplace. From the number of requests I receive for topics related to laughter, joy, happiness and peace of mind, it is obvious that there is a serious problem out there when it comes to living full, happy and relaxed lives.

I believe that life is meant to be enjoyed in spite of the pain and suffering that exist in abundance. Life is fundamentally a mystery to be lived and celebrated, not a problem to be solved and endured. There is something terribly wrong when the World Health Organization predicts that by the year 2020 A.D. depression will be the leading cause of disability throughout the world. There is something wrong when sleeping pills and tranquilizers are devoured by the truckload throughout North America; when children, in ever increasing numbers, are plagued with attention deficit disorder; when stories of spousal abuse, child abuse, road rage, substance abuse and youth violence fill the pages of newspapers daily.

We have lost the art of joyful, peaceful living. The question is, "How are we going to rediscover it?" I don't profess to have the answers to all the complex social and psychological problems confronting society today. I will leave this task to those more qualified, although the experts don't seem to have any answers either. I just want to address what we as individuals can do to live more effectively and enthusiastically in this chaotic world.

If there is any truth to the adage that, while we have no control over what happens to us in life, we do have total control over our attitude toward what happens to us, then this is the place to start. Change our attitudes and we can change our lives.

I don't want to let governments go unchallenged. They do have a responsibility to invest heavily in the well-being of their citizens. But the fact remains that we, as individuals, must take control of our lives to ensure that we do everything in our power to maximize achievement and to actualize our tremendous potential.

Brian Tracy, in his book, "Maximum Achievement" says that happiness and peace of mind are the highest goods in life and achieving both should be our central task to which all others should be subservient.

I would like to share some of the techniques and strategies I have found effective in creating happiness and peace of mind in my own life. Once again I want to remind you that we are less interested in achieving perfection in what we do, and more interested in progress.

STRATEGIES FOR ACHIEVING HAPPINESS AND PEACE OF MIND

THOUGHT REPLACEMENT:

If we choose our thoughts and we are able to think of only one thing at a time then to be happy and at peace choose happy and peaceful thoughts. It sounds easy and it is, in theory. The problem arises in keeping the mind, which tends to be like a racehorse, focused on the thought selected. As difficult as this is at first, it does become easier with practice.

VISUALIZATION:

I find it helpful to use visualization to replace negative, stressful and unhappy thoughts. I visualize, in my mind, the thought I want to dismiss actually leaving my body and a new, happy or peaceful thought entering and remaining.

MEDITATION AND RELAXATION:

Doctor Herbert Benson in his book, "The Relaxation Response" outlines the physical and psychological benefits of relaxation as well as various methods and techniques used to invoke the relaxation response. Each method is effective and produces similar results. Whether you use meditation, progressive relaxation, deep breathing or self-hypnosis, it doesn't matter. What you want to do is induce the alpha state and reap its benefits. All of these methods accomplish this.

I use meditation to go for alpha. I find that it helps me effectively dwell on one thought to the exclusion of all others.

AFFIRMATIONS:

When in the relaxed or alpha state I give myself positive suggestions or affirmations related to the attitude I want to change or the emotion I want to experience. The important word here is 'positive'. Never use negative phrases like, " I will not think such and such." It is much more effective to say, "I will think such and such." Also, keep your affirmations and suggestions in the present tense, e.g. "I am becoming more peaceful every moment" rather than, "I will become more peaceful." Remember that we tend to become what we constantly affirm.

HUMOUR:

In everything we do, try to see and enjoy the humour in it all. Never forget that life is too serious to be taken seriously. Once again, be gentle with yourself and laugh a lot.

LIVE BETTER... LAUGH A LOT.

READING ABOUT THESE IDEAS DOES NOTHING
BUT INCREASE YOUR AWARENESS.
TO BRING ABOUT THE CHANGE YOU DESIRE
TAKES TIME, EFFORT, AND PRACTICE.
TAKE TIME, MAKE THE EFFORT AND
PRACTISE DAILY AND GREAT THINGS
WILL BEGIN TO HAPPEN.

HOW STRESSED ARE YOU?

CHECK THE ITEMS THAT APPLY TO YOU.

- ☐ SPEAK RAPIDLY
- ☐ INTERRUPT OTHERS
- ☐ EAT TOO QUICKLY
- ☐ HATE WASTING TIME
- ☐ IMPATIENT WITH OTHERS
- ☐ NEVER SEEM TO CATCH UP
- ☐ SCHEDULE MORE THAN I HAVE TIME FOR
- ☐ DRIVE TOO FAST WHEN I'M NOT LATE
- ☐ ALWAYS WANT TO WIN
- ☐ NO TIME FOR REST AND RELAXATION
- ☐ CAN'T SEEM TO SIT STILL
- ☐ NO TIME FOR INTIMACY
- ☐ FEARFUL AND ANXIOUS

THE MORE ITEMS YOU HAVE APPLYING TO YOU THE MORE STRESSED YOU ARE.

SEEKING SIMPLE PLEASURES

Paul Pearsall, in his work on pleasure, advocates the enjoyment of simple pleasures or E.S.P., an art we seem to have lost in this hustle bustle world.

Miracles are all around us if we would only take the time to see and enjoy. I think Blake's opening lines of *Auguries of Innocence* say it best, "To see a world in a grain of sand, and heaven in a wild flower, hold infinity in the palm of your hand and eternity in an hour."

Last night there was a full moon over Lake Huron. We sat around the campfire basking in the moon's gentle brilliance enjoying one another in the miracle of summer moonlight. It just doesn't get any better than this. A perfect example of E.S.P.

HANDLING STRESS EFFECTIVELY

DO YOU...

GIVE YOURSELF TIME IN ORDER TO AVOID RUSHING?	YES	NO
GO THROUGH THE DAY AT A COMFORTABLE PACE?	YES	NO
ENJOY THE SCENIC ROUTE TO WORK EVEN IF IT IS LONGER?	YES	NO
DO THINGS FOR THE SHEER JOY OF DOING THEM?	YES	NO
AVOID GETTING UPSET AT THE FAULTS OF OTHERS?	YES	NO
ENJOY RELATIONSHIPS FOR THEIR OWN SAKE ?	YES	NO
FEEL CONFIDENT STANDING UP FOR YOURSELF?	YES	NO
ACCEPT PEOPLE AS THEY ARE?	YES	NO
FEEL REASONABLY SATISFIED WITH YOURSELF?	YES	NO
ACCEPT THE THINGS IN LIFE YOU CANNOT CHANGE?	YES	NO

THE GREATER NUMBER OF YES ANSWERS, THE MORE EFFECTIVE YOU ARE AT HANDLING STRESS.

WHAT'S THE RUSH?

Have you ever found yourself rushing to get somewhere when you have all the time in the world to get there? It's almost as if we have been programmed to move quickly under any and all circumstances.

When your body and mind are in passing gear constantly it isn't healthy. Your blood pressure rises, your heart races and you become stressed and ready for action, whether action is required or not.

When I find myself in this situation, rushing like mad for no good reason, I consciously direct myself to slow down. I actually make my body move in a more relaxed and efficient manner. I breathe deeply and slowly and focus my attention on flowers, the sky, trees, anything that speaks to me of a more natural rhythm. It works, and could become habitual.

Do I still find myself rushing? Of course, but much less frequently, and when I do I can count on strategies that are effective in enabling me to return to sanity.

Never be so busy trying to get somewhere that you fail to see where you've been

Anyone too busy to invest time in maintaining friendships, is busier than they should be.

SIGNS OF INNER PEACE

(Paraphrased from Wayne Dyer)

People with peace of mind...

...are more loving and caring.

...smile more often.

...have a keen sense of gratitude for all that is.

...feel a strong link with others and with nature.

...worry less.

...live in the present and enjoy each moment of their lives.

...are less judgmental.

...have fewer fears.

...act spontaneously.

MEDITATION

WHAT IS MEDITATION?

Meditation is an ancient method of achieving tranquility and peace of mind. It involves dwelling on a sound, phrase, or image exclusively.

WHAT ARE THE BENEFITS OF MEDITATION?

Meditation increases your awareness, promotes serenity, relieves stress, and helps you cope with the problems of life. It also has been shown to lower blood pressure and help overcome insomnia.

IT IS IMPORTANT TO REALIZE THAT MEDITATION IS NOT PSYCHOTHERAPY, AND WILL NOT SOLVE DEEP ROOTED PROBLEMS.

HOW DO YOU MEDITATE?

Sit in a comfortable chair.

Select your focus (sound, phrase, or image). Your image can be a flame, flower, quiet beach, etc. It is your choice. Don't let anyone or any group try to tell you that you require a specific image, sound or phrase only they can provide (always for a fee, of course). Some people prefer to concentrate on their breathing. Remember it's the process of focusing not the object of your focus that is important.

Close your eyes.

Begin to hold your focus.

Distractions will come. Let them. Don't try to resist their presence. Just visualize them leaving your mind and return to your focus.

Meditate for just a few minutes in the beginning gradually increasing the time to 15 or 20 minutes. Some suggest that you meditate twice a day. Sometimes I manage to get two sessions in, but most of the time I meditate once a day for about 30 minutes.

HOW WILL YOU KNOW THAT YOU ARE MEDITATING?

You will have a deep feeling of peace, detachment, relaxation and tranquility.

Slow me down, Lord

Ease the pounding of my heart by the quieting of my mind.

Steady my hurried pace with a vision of the eternal reach of time.

Give me, amid the confusion of my day, the calmness of the everlasting hills.

Break the tension of my nerves and muscles with the music of the singing streams that live in my memory.

Help me know the magical, restoring power of sleep.

Teach me the art of taking minute vacations, of slowing down to look at a flower, to chat with a friend, to pet a dog, to read a few lines from a good book.

Slow me down, Lord, and inspire me to send my roots deep into the soil of life's enduring values that I may grow toward the stars of my greater destiny.

(Author unknown)

THE MIND IS A WILD STALLION THAT MUST BE TAMED.... BE PATIENT.

ATTITUDE IS EVERYTHING

If we are the products of our attitudes then it is very important for us to examine our attitudes both positive and negative to discover the impact they are having on our lives. This is even more important if we are determined to maximize the potential that is ours, a potential which, in the vast majority of us, remains grossly underdeveloped.

Positive attitudes release a power to achieve that will astound you, while negative attitudes severely hamper our becoming the people we are capable of becoming. It becomes the central task of anyone interested in actualizing their potential to become involved in the process of attitudinal transformation.

Attitudinal transformation takes time, effort and determination but it can be done. Don't expect perfection, just progress. It took a long time to develop negative attitudes, and it will take time to transform them. It is also important not to concentrate on more than one or two negative attitudes at once. If you overload your agenda for change you run the risk of becoming discouraged and giving up.

Once you have identified the negative attitude you wish to transform, commit yourself to the process of becoming conscious of that attitude cropping up throughout the day. You will be surprised at how quickly you will become aware of your target attitude. When you are focused on the attitude, visualize it leaving your body and flying off into the great beyond. Now replace it with a positive attitude and give yourself the suggestion that from now on this will be your dominant thought pattern.

Whenever your old negative attitude creeps back into your mind engage this process of thought replacement. Soon the new attitude will become dominant and you will find yourself enjoying its positive power in your life.

Be gentle with yourself when you fall back into the old pattern of thinking. Believe that the change you desire will come more frequently and it will. It might help to remember that human beings use only ten percent of their mind potential so you have a huge reservoir of unused potential to help you over any periods of discouragement.

Don't forget to use humour to keep your spirits up and put the entire process into perspective. **HUMOUR MAKES IT HAPPEN.**

Here are a few selected pieces of wit and wisdom to help keep you going.

"The mind can make a heaven out of hell or a hell out of heaven."   Milton

Two men looked out from behind prison bars,
One saw mud, the other saw stars.

We choose the attitude with which we face our fate.
V.Frankl

ATTITUDE IS EVERYTHING

You don't see things the way they are, you see things the way you are.
    The Talmud

The greatest tragedy in life is not in how much we suffer, but in how much we miss.
    T. Carlyle

You wouldn't worry about what people thought of you if you only knew how seldom they did.

Pain and suffering are a lot like gas, they too will pass.

We are what we think about all day long.

Wherever you may go in life, whatever be your goal, keep your eye upon the doughnut and not upon the hole.

Fill your days with little joys.

Everything you have become or will become is the result of the way you think.

We can all learn a great deal from the story of the attractive, confident nurse who deducted ten beats per minute from the pulse of every male patient.

After examining the knee of an 80 year old patient, the doctor concluded that the pain she was experiencing was simply due to age. The patient looked at the doctor and said, "But my other knee is the same age and it doesn't hurt."

Language declares to the world the attitudes we possess. Proof ? An old car is a classic; an old object is an antique; an old man is a fart.

I have a love/hate relationship with dandelions. The environmentalist in me wants to make them welcome in my lawn, while the urban gardener in me wants to rid the world of the menace. One day a friend of mine, who happened to be a retired science teacher and committed environmentalist said to me, "Mike, I've solved the problem of dandelions in my lawn without compromising the environment." When I eagerly asked him how, he replied, "I've learned to love them." Now that's a shift in attitude.

If you wish to take control of your life and achieve your potential you must learn to control your thoughts.

Someone once said that to expect life to treat you fairly because you're a good person, is like expecting a bull not to charge you because you're a vegetarian.

I like the story of the 83 year old woman who, upon looking into the mirror at her wrinkled face, remarked, "They're not making mirrors like they used to."

Worry is like a rocking chair; it will give you something to do, but it won't get you anywhere.

When Agatha Christie was asked how she liked being married to an archeologist, she replied that it was wonderful because the older she got the more interested in her he became.

It helps to cultivate a strong sense of the ridiculous in life.

The main business of life is to enjoy it.

For every ailment under the sun, there is a cure or there is none. If there is one try to find it. If there is none, never mind it.

If we focus on decline and decay as we age, it is quite possible that we will reap what we focus on.

Abraham Lincoln once said that we will be as happy as we make up our mind to be.

We must try to recapture the sense of joy, wonder and celebration we had, in abundance, as children.

> *"I want to die living, not live dying."*
> *Harold Kushner*

Charles Dubois once said that we must be prepared, at a moment's notice, to sacrifice who we are, for who we are capable of becoming.

Act the way you want to become and you will become the way you act.

While we have very little control over what happens to us in life, we do have control over what we do with what happens to us.

When you change your attitudes you can change your life because our behaviour flows from our attitudes.

ATTITUDINAL HEALING

WE LIVE OUT OF OUR ATTITUDES.

WE CHOOSE OUR ATTITUDES.

WE CAN CHANGE OUR ATTITUDES.

CHANGE YOUR ATTITUDES
AND
CHANGE YOUR LIFE .

REMEMBER,
YOUR HEADACHE
IS GOOD NEWS TO
AN ASPIRIN
SALESPERSON!
HEADACHE
AHEAD
ASPIRIN
CO.

SOME PEOPLE AREN'T CHEERFUL...

THEY'RE JUST PROUD OF THEIR TEETH!

When adults say, "It's happy hour..." does that mean all the other hours are unhappy?

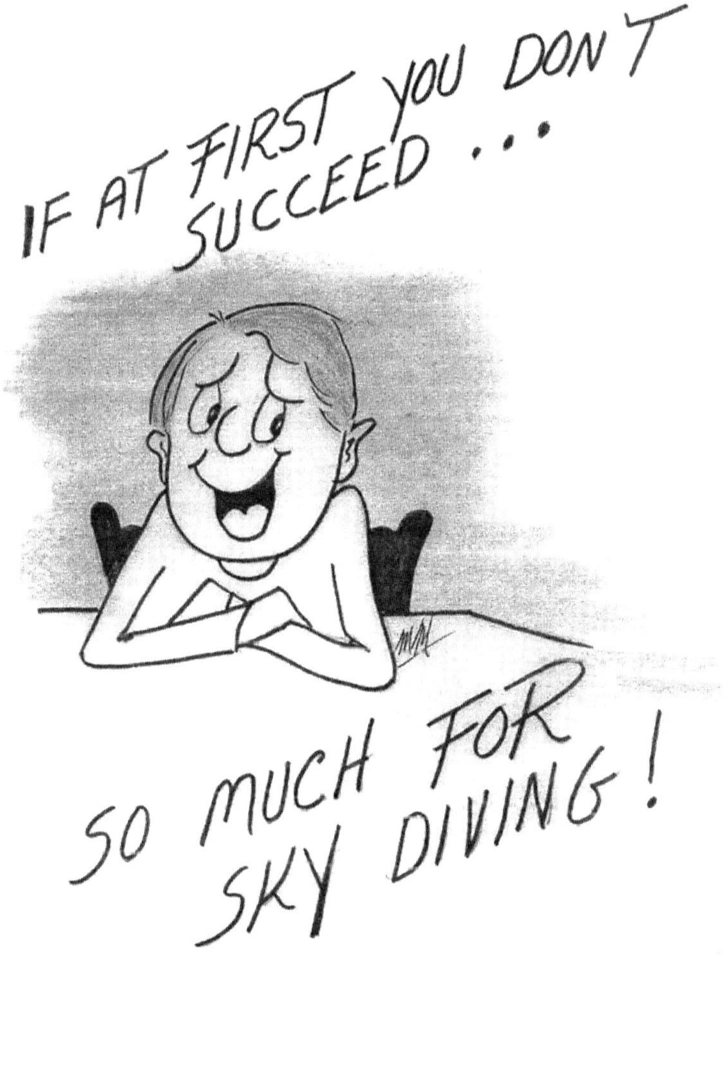
IF AT FIRST YOU DON'T SUCCEED . . .
SO MUCH FOR SKY DIVING!

I USED TO RESPOND TO MOST THINGS PEOPLE SAID, WITH, "BALONEY" AND I HAD VERY FEW FRIENDS. THEN I CHANGED AND RESPONDED, "MARVELOUS" AND NOW I'M INVITED EVERYWHERE!

SELF ESTEEM

John Powell wrote that we are the sum total of all who have loved us or who have failed to love us. If this is true, and it seems reasonable to assume it is, then it is no wonder that we have such an extensive self-esteem problem. The very people who should be affirming our uniqueness and dignity are often the ones who seem to delight in putting us down, often in jest.

While I am a strong advocate of humour I realize that it can be used to crush the human spirit as well as heal it. Sarcasm, ridicule and put downs can destroy our confidence and decimate our ability to actualize our potential. Why do we persist in putting people down? Is it an attempt to make ourselves look good? I think so.

When I was seventeen I was six feet three inches tall and weighed 129 pounds of rippling muscle. I looked like a broom with glasses. One day I was combing my hair in a full length mirror when my aunt walked by and said, "You know, Mike, it's a damn good thing God gave you personality because He sure didn't give you looks." She laughed, thinking she was really funny while I stood there shocked and hurt.

The sad thing is that she is probably unaware of the impact her words had on me and possibly unaware of even having said them. To this day when my wife says that I look handsome I am always tempted to say, "Don't get carried away. I'm clean and I smell good but that's about it."

Once hurtful words leave your mouth it is impossible to retrieve them and their negative, destructive impact can remain for years. While everyone is guilty of this from time to time, we must remain committed to eliminating this kind of destructive speech from our relationships.

THE POWER OF FORGIVENESS

As human beings we don't always behave the way we should. Often we do and say things that hurt the people we love the most. Can we eliminate this kind of hurt from our relationships? Probably not. Can we minimize their occurrence and cushion their caustic impact on our loved ones? Definitely!

I don't want to be the kind of person who hurts others whether they are close to me or not. I have dedicated myself to positive, affirming relationships and I am prepared to do what it takes to ensure that I move in this direction. What do I do when I fail as I inevitably do periodically? I ask for forgiveness by simply saying "I'm sorry." I realize that many find these two little words difficult to utter, but there is magic, healing and power in the utterance. Once forgiveness is received I recommit myself to the task of becoming the kind of person I desperately want to be. The problem I have is that in a bad week I find myself saying "I'm sorry" too often. But I'm working on it.

I recall dumping verbally on our son Chris a few years ago for no other reason than I was in one of those moods. After I came to my senses I looked at him and said, "I'm sorry son, you didn't deserve that." He looked at me and said, "It's O.K. Dad, don't worry about it." His quickness to forgive impressed me and I remarked, "You forgive so easily Chris. How do you do it?" "Living with you gives me a lot of practise," he replied. OUCH!

In John Powell's book, *Why am I Afraid to Tell You Who I Am?* he answers this question with, "because who I am is all I've got and I'm afraid you won't like me." How we long to be loved, accepted and appreciated.

I'm not who I think I am and I'm not who you think I am. I am who I think you think I am. Sink your teeth into that for awhile.

There was a rather interesting study done a few years ago by Colorado State University. Two hundred and fifty people were surveyed regarding receiving compliments. The results were revealing. Of the 250 surveyed two thirds said they were very uncomfortable receiving compliments. One half stated that they felt obligated to return the compliment. Thirty percent said that they would appear conceited if they didn't try to neutralize the compliment, and twenty percent suspected ulterior motives on the part of the one giving the compliment. Why can't we just relax, enjoy the affirmation and say, "Thank you."

HUMILITY?

There I was standing in front of an audience of about two hundred people speaking on the subject of self-esteem. I wanted people to see that each of us is a gifted, talented child of the universe. It was also my intention to illustrate that most of us are very comfortable sharing our perceived shortcomings and very uncomfortable sharing openly our talents and gifts.

I began my presentation by saying, "You are looking at a very gifted human being." I proceeded to outline my gifts. When I had finished I received the response I was seeking when a woman looked at me and said, "Well humility sure as hell isn't one of them." Her response reflected what most of us feel when someone articulates in public the things they do well or the things of which they are proud. She was very uncomfortable and immediately thought I was bragging.

In essence, humility isn't thinking little of yourself, it is thinking of yourself little. And you can only forget yourself in the service of others when you love yourself and appreciate the many gifts you have been given. When this is achieved you will eagerly sit and listen to another share their giftedness and applaud their place in the universe, without feeling threatened or uncomfortable. It becomes one gifted human being affirming and appreciating another.

SELF TALK

If we are the products of our own self talk then it is vital that what we tell ourselves about ourselves is positive and contributes to our continued growth and formation. If you are like me you tend to focus on your limitations in certain situations. I happen to have a number of gifts of which I am very proud, as we all do. But being a handy Mr. Fix-it around the house is definitely not one of them. When a job needs to be done, rather than approaching it with a relaxed confidence, I immediately begin to hyperventilate. I tell myself that the task is impossible because I was born without the Mr. Fix-it gene.

At this point I usually call our friend Brian who just happened to be born with one hundred thousand more fix-it genes than anyone else on the planet. Whenever Brian fixes a problem for me and I see that it didn't take a degree in nuclear physics, I say to myself, " I could have done that."

Saying it is easy, believing it is another matter.

Away from the fix-it front I have the ability to speak positively to myself, but we all have at least one area of vulnerability that needs our attention. Perhaps one day, before I die, I will be able to take something apart and actually know how to put it back together again. At present I can only take things apart.

It bothers me when I hear people say that they have no talent or that they're falling apart or their mind is turning to mush. Such negative self talk conditions us to limitation when we should be conditioned to endless possibility

If psychologists are correct in their belief that we use only 10 percent of our mind's potential, then I want to concentrate on actualizing the remaining 90 percent. We can begin by committing ourselves to the elimination of negative self talk from our lives and replacing it with self talk that unleashes the enormous power of our potential.

When you find yourself aware of negative, self limiting language in your life whether it is triggered by yourself, others or the culture in which you live, stop for a moment, dismiss it and replace it with a positive, empowering statement. Remember that harsh negative criticism, whether self imposed or imposed by others, is destructive and serves no real purpose in your growth as a human being. Challenging yourself to become what you are capable of becoming is one thing, condemning yourself for not measuring up, often to impossible standards, is another.

Whether your negative self talk involves perceived physical, social, intellectual, emotional or artistic limitations, be assured that just because you hold a certain negative perception doesn't mean that the perception is accurate. The more frequently you articulate destructive self perceptions the more entrenched these faulty perceptions become and the more difficult it becomes to erase them from your mind.

BE PATIENT... I'M IN PROCESS!

POSITIVE SELF TALK

OLD IS ALL IN THE MIND.
LIVE IN THE MOMENT.
GO FOR THE GUSTO.
LIVE LIFE TO THE FULLEST.
EACH DAY IS A GIFT.
KEEP ON KEEPING ON.
LIFE IS AN ADVENTURE.
KEEP LAUGHING.
DIE LIVING, DON'T LIVE DYING.
FILL EACH DAY WITH SIMPLE JOYS.
LIVE AND LET LIVE.
I LIVE IN AWE OF THE BEAUTY AROUND ME.
LIFE IS WORTH LIVING.

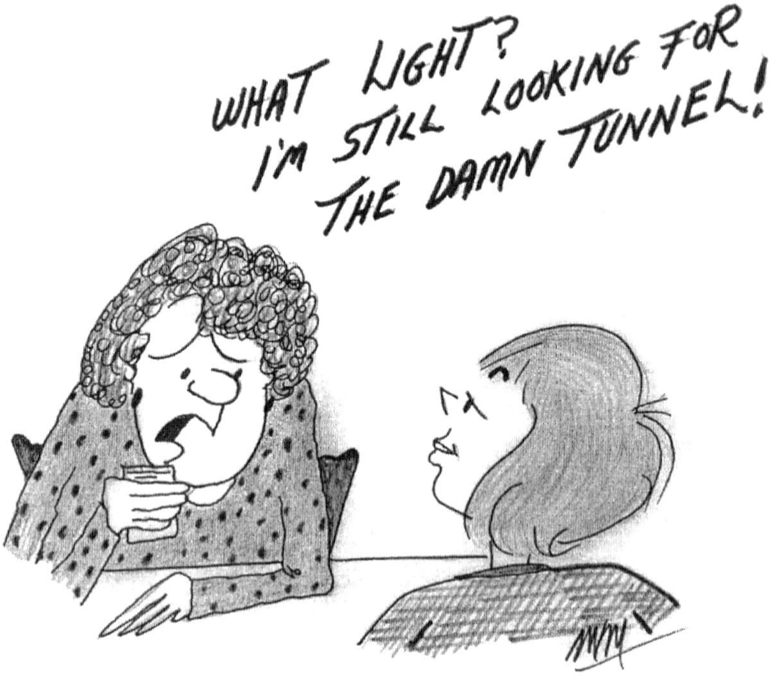
WHAT LIGHT? I'M STILL LOOKING FOR THE DAMN TUNNEL!

NEGATIVE SELF TALK

I'M OVER THE HILL.

TOO OLD TO CUT THE MUSTARD.

GETTING OLD IS FOR THE BIRDS

I'M READY FOR THE HOME.

TIME IS TAKING ITS TOLL.

JUST PUTTING IN TIME.

NOTHING ON ME SEEMS TO WORK ANY MORE.

LIVING ON BORROWED TIME.

I'M NO SPRING CHICKEN.

WHAT CAN YOU EXPECT AT OUR AGE?

I HAVE NO TALENT.

I AM USELESS.

THERE'S MORE SIDEWALK BEHIND ME THAN AHEAD OF ME.

FEAR

Gerald Jampolsky suggests in his book, *Love is Letting Go of Fear* that most, if not all negative human behaviour flows from fear. Therefore confronting and controlling fear should be high on any agenda for self actualization.

Fear can cripple us emotionally, for if we fear excessively we risk losing the joy of living. If we fear getting old we can become obsessed with the pursuit of youth. Such a serious pre-occupation places our primary focus on ourselves to the exclusion of our other relationships. Fear turns us inward when we are called to live outward lives.

If I fear being dominated and outnumbered by immigrants I can easily become racist losing the sense of unity with all people on the planet.

Fear of public speaking, which is supposed to be the number one fear in the minds of North Americans, could prevent you from sharing your thoughts and opinions freely and confidently, to the detriment of the community in which you live. The free expression of personal opinion is vital to the democratic process.

Fear of illness can actually result in making what we fear become a reality. There is nothing more dangerous to our health than the fear of losing it.

The obsessive dread of gaining weight can result in eating disorders which can destroy individual lives and families.

Closely related to this is the fear of not measuring up to society's image of the perfect body. When you feel that your body is inadequate you can become obsessed by a futile quest for perfection which can lead to breast implants, breast reduction, face lifts, tummy tucks, hair transplants liposuction etc. The goal of becoming your best self gets lost in a misguided search for a youthful, fat free, surgically sculpted anatomy. What is so terribly wrong with loving who you are, body, mind and spirit, at every stage of your life? We seem to have a cultural bias against getting old and looking it.

Fear is a serious barrier to becoming and must be dealt with if we are to live full, happy, healthy lives. I have outlined a few techniques which I have found effective in my own confrontation with fear. You may find them helpful.

- In a relaxed state visualize yourself confronting and overcoming a specific fear.

- Force yourself to do what you fear the most and your fear will eventually vanish.

- Repeat frequently, "Most of what I fear will never happen."

- If you are a religious person search your Scripture for quotations which speak of overcoming fear. e.g.

    "*Why are you frightened? Are you still without faith?*"
    Mark 4:40

    "*Don't be afraid, only believe.*" Mark 5:36

    (These are just two examples from the Christian Scripture. Whatever your holy book is I know you will find similar references to fear which will give you courage, comfort and insight.)

I FEAR...
DEATH - LIFE
AGING - WATER
HEIGHTS - MICE
LOSS OF HAIR
SICKNESS
SPEED - BUGS
REJECTION
LONELINESS
PUBLIC
SPEAKING
INTIMACY
SAYING NO
ASKING FOR
WHAT I WANT...
M.M.

QUOTATIONS ON FEAR

"Of all base passions, fear is the most accursed."
　　　William Shakespeare

"Do the thing you fear, and the death of fear is certain."
　　　Emerson

"Nothing is so much to be feared as fear."
　　　Thoreau

"One of the great discoveries a man makes, one of his greatest surprises, is to find out he can do what he was afraid he couldn't do."
　　　Henry Ford

"Nothing in life is to be feared. It is only to be understood."
　　　Marie Curie

"Action conquers fear."
　　　Peter Nivio Zarlenga

"Fear is met and destroyed with courage."
　　　J.F. Bell

When I write about overcoming fear, I am referring to the fear we experience in our daily lives which has not become obsessive. Any fear that is preventing us from living productive lives requires professional care.

I FINALLY SAW THE LIGHT AT THE END OF THE TUNNEL
ONLY TO DISCOVER ...
IT WAS A FREIGHT TRAIN.
MM

WELLNESS

It seems that everywhere we turn today we hear talk of paradigms and paradigm shifts and their impact on us in the workplace, at home, school, church etc. But just what are paradigms, how do they impact on our lives, and why do they have to be shifting at all?

The word paradigm comes from the Greek word *paradigma* which means pattern. So paradigms are patterns of thinking which influence our behaviour. Human behaviour flows out of existing religious, social, educational, economic and medical paradigms.

Change in a culture results when people feel that something within an existing pattern of thinking doesn't work any longer. For example, parents feel that their children cannot read the way they should be able to and they determine that change is required within the educational paradigm to guarantee improved literacy. In other words, a paradigm shift is required. Often there is disagreement regarding the direction of the paradigm shift, with some wanting to return to the paradigm of the "good old days" and some wanting to explore new patterns based on a blend of what worked before and new contemporary research. In any event, no change occurs unless there is dissatisfaction or discomfort.

For my purposes I want to concentrate on the shifting medical paradigm taking place throughout North America and the world. People are moving toward a complimentary health paradigm and away from the traditional impersonal doctor centered curative model.

We are no longer satisfied to be the kidney or the appendix in room 122, who places total trust in the expertise of the medical practitioner. Experience teaches us that this pattern of thinking just doesn't work any longer.

It is quite obvious that we are moving from a disease, doctor, curative medical paradigm, to a more personalized, patient centered, partnership pattern. People are now taking responsibility for their own health. We want to work as a team with our doctors and the medical establishment in the promotion of our health and wellness. We are witnessing the rise of the autonomous health seeker who wants to incorporate the best of traditional medicine with the best of what complimentary medicine has to offer.

At first medical science was skeptical about the move to complimentary medicine, but now we see a reluctant willingness on the part of the medical establishment to, at least, be open to avenues of healing previously considered quackery. If enough people believe something long enough chances are that there must be something valid to what they believe.

So now we have people involved in such healing therapies as herbalism, biofeedback, visualization, humour therapy, hypnotherapy, relaxation and meditation. Great results have been recorded when patients, working in conjunction with their doctors, have included a complimentary therapy in their treatment. It seems clear that the future of medical science will involve a combination of curative, preventative and promotional approaches. Promotional medicine concerns itself with just how much healthier we can get and according to many authorities on the subject, our health potential is incredible.

In fact there are those who believe that, with proper nutrition, exercise, attitude and medical supervision, humans could live active healthy lives beyond the century mark.

I am quite contented to add quality to whatever time I have on this earth. If, in the process, I end up living a long, healthy and active life I will certainly consider it a most welcome bonus.

LIVE, LAUGH, LOVE AND BE HAPPY

For the next 24 hours, deliberately speak and think positive thoughts about people and events.

Look for the good in people.

Make time to relax. Think of a peaceful scene and let it quiet your mind and your body.

Listen to soothing music.

Don't take yourself or others too seriously.

Remember that good health requires a healthy mind and a healthy body.

Don't let the faults and weaknesses of others upset you.

Health of mind, body and spirit is within your control.

Learn to laugh, and let laughter heal your body and spirit.

Love your work and enjoy it. Change your attitude toward your work and the people at your place of employment and joy will return to your life in great measure.

Count your blessings each day.

Love others as they are, and not as you want them to be.

Remember that worry and fear are destructive emotions. They rob you of happiness and joy. Let go of worry and fear and place your trust in a power greater than yourself.

Foster an attitude of appreciation.

Live fully, laugh heartily, relax daily, love deeply and enjoy the journey.

TO CULTIVATE JOY...

1. Choose positive attitudes.
2. Seek out and enjoy peaceful places.
3. Slow down and smell the roses.
4. Meditate at least once a day.
5. Delight in music.
6. Be open about your feelings.
7. Listen attentively to others.
8. Laugh easily and often.
9. Don't be afraid to cry.
10. Concentrate on what is beautiful in life.
11. Try to understand the negatives of life.
12. Stay away from miserable people.
13. Listen to your inner voice.
14. Cultivate an attitude of gratitude.

15. Embrace the mystery of life.

16. Foster a sense of awe and wonder.

LIFE IS A MYSTERY TO BE LIVED, NOT A PROBLEM TO BE SOLVED.

Some people bring joy wherever they go... some, whenever they leave!

FRIENDSHIP

I have very few close male friends. There are many men with whom I associate and whose company I do enjoy, but there are only two who really know me and with whom I feel free and comfortable to speak at an intimate level.

I often wish things were different because I'm the kind of person who needs to talk about life, love, hopes, books and ideas. Most men feel uncomfortable sharing deeply, or feel compelled to compete within conversation rather than listen and attend.

Women, on the other hand, generally, have less difficulty with in-depth conversation. Perhaps that's why I enjoy the friendship and company of women.

A LESSON IN FRIENDSHIP

The greatest lesson in friendship was taught to me years ago by a loyal and trusted friend. Burt and I became friends early in high school and have remained so for almost 40 years. When I graduated and went off to Teachers' College I developed many new friends and sadly, forgot the old.

One day I received a letter from Burt firmly challenging me never to discard old friends in the formation of new. When I returned home to Sault Ste. Marie for the holidays my lesson continued. I'm happy to say that I learned my lesson well.

Make new friends, but keep the old. One is silver, the other gold.

MALE BONDING

I think men have been short-changed when it comes to friendship. We talk about male bonding, but we never really bond in the real sense of the word. Men get together over a few beers and tell jokes, talk about sports, cars, computers and women (not necessarily in that order) but never speak of their feelings and fears.

I was in the company of a group of men who had come together to support a mutual friend who was going through a rough time. Nothing was ever shared about feelings and fears until one night a member mentioned that he feared aging and death. The response was predictable, "Come on, lighten up and have another beer."

We do a disservice to our young males when we continue to socialize them to be tough, emotionally aloof and closed about their feelings. The truth is that all men have fears, frustrations and the need to weep. We need to connect with other men at a much deeper level than, "How about those Blue Jays?"

PATIENCE

I am not a patient man. I want to be, but I'm not. It has been a constant struggle to become what I am not, patient. I am pleased to report that I have come a long way in overcoming my impatience but the struggle continues daily. My wife, Carol, would say that I am 60% more patient than I was in the first ten years of our marriage, and she should know seeing that she has borne the brunt of my impatience, and has done so with class and admirable forbearance.

I love people, but hate crowds, lineups, and traffic jams. The thought of standing behind a person at the grocery checkout who hands the cashier a handful of coupons and then says, "Is there anything in there I can use?" drives me crazy. It really irks me to be next in line at the local doughnut shop behind someone ordering four dozen assorted doughnuts who pauses between each selection for what seems to Mr. Patience like an eternity. My impatience becomes tangible in church when I am made to crawl over an entire family in a pew because they refuse to move over to let me in. So much for loving your neighbour. At this point I'm sure you will all agree with my wife that I am not, by temperament, a patient man.

After years of fuming, fretting, seething, swearing and blaming my wife and children for every impatient episode in which I found myself, I decided to change. I would love to be able to say that I am always Captain Calm in every situation but that would be untrue. What I can say truthfully is that I am committed to staying calm and patient under stress, and I have discovered a set of skills that help me do just that.

From the reports I receive from the front line whatever I'm doing is working effectively.

"How do you do it?" you ask. Let me tell you.

DOCTOR CALM'S PRESCRIPTION FOR PATIENCE

When under stress...

TALK CALMLY TO YOURSELF.
I find saying something like, "Slow down, Michael, you're going to have a stroke if you keep this up," works well for me. I personally find the threat of death or permanent disability extremely motivating.

BREATHE DEEPLY AND SLOWLY.

REPEAT FREQUENTLY, "EVERY DAY, IN EVERY WAY, I AM BECOMING MORE PATIENT."

CONSCIOUSLY RELAX YOUR FACIAL MUSCLES.
When you are impatient you tighten the muscles of the face giving you that "ticked off" look. When you relax your facial muscles calmness seems to return. Simply tell the muscles to relax, visualize them doing so and it happens.

MENTALLY PICTURE YOURSELF ON A BEACH WATCHING A GORGEOUS SUNSET.
The waves gently massage your toes causing your entire body to feel deeply relaxed. You are given an ice cold drink to sip while soft music fills the air. It just doesn't get any better than this.

MEMORIZE THIS LINE .
"SLOW ME DOWN, LORD. EASE THE POUNDING OF MY HEART BY THE QUIETING OF MY MIND."

LISTEN TO BEAUTIFUL MUSIC ON YOUR CAR RADIO.
Let it soothe the savage beast.

THIS PROCESS WORKS... BE PATIENT!

PIZZAZZ

I am drawn to people with pizzazz, that spark of enthusiasm and excitement about life that makes being in their presence a joy. They smile easily and often and laugh with great energy and pleasure. It feels good to be alive and in their company.

People with pizzazz don't have to be loud or boisterous. They can be quietly positive and enthusiastic, appreciating the moment with whomever they happen to share it. They listen, care and respond generously. They are gifts.

The late Leo Buscaglia, a man who possessed pizzazz in abundance, tells of meeting a woman who was lacking this gift. She had a perpetual frown on her face and was miserable most of the time. Leo looked at her and asked how she was feeling. She glanced back and said curtly, "Just fine." "Good, now if you would only tell that to your face," Leo replied.

LANGUAGE AND REALITY

Language does define our reality, but never adequately. While words are all we have to express how we feel and what we think, we are always left with the lingering sense that they don't always do the job.

I remember asking a friend to describe the pain of childbirth. She thought for awhile and then said, "It's rather like being hit across the back full force with a 2x4 inch board." Then she added, "Try thinking about what it would feel like to pass a watermelon." Since I have never experienced either, thank God, and because the pain involved varies depending on the pain threshold of the mother, I still have no real understanding of the pain involved in giving birth to a child.

The inadequacies of language become more apparent when coupled with the discomfort I feel when visiting a funeral home. When a grieving family member says, "Thanks for coming, it means so much to us," I inevitably respond with something like, "It's my pleasure," much to the chagrin of my wife. At times like these words just don't effectively express the sorrow and the anguish we feel in our hearts. But words are all we have as inadequate as they are. Perhaps we should say nothing and just put a caring comforting arm around the one suffering the loss.

ENLIGHTENED MALADJUSTMENT

Psychiatrists say that we should be normal and well- adjusted. It sounds reasonable until you examine closely how society defines normal and well-adjusted.

Our normal and well-adjusted multitudes are so anxious, depressed and angry, that they consume sleeping pills to achieve what was meant to be achieved naturally and tranquilizers to restore calmness to our culturally induced turmoil.

While many would agree that anger, depression and anxiety result from the lifestyle we have come to accept as normal, no one can agree on how to stop the collective insanity. We have created a monster.

Doctor Paul Pearsall advocates that individuals should, in their quest for health and well being, consciously opt out of this socially induced frenzy and commit themselves to the path of enlightened maladjustment. In other words we should make pleasure, laughter, joy, spontaneity and freedom our primary values. Doing something wild, weird and wonderful for the sheer fun of it promotes health and well being and fills our lives with joy. I think he has a point here. Don't you?

The problem is that while you are out there doing all these wild, weird and wonderfully spontaneous things, everyone else is thinking you have lost all your marbles.

AGING AND DEATH

My wife Carol and I are at an age when we find ourselves attending many more funerals than weddings. It seems that every time we read the obituaries we are off to the funeral home. It certainly makes us confront our own mortality.

Every time I visit my 83 year old mother she talks in terms of who is gone, who is about to go, and who should be gone but is still hanging on. We have been told many times that death is a part of life, but are we really prepared to accept it?

I believe that one can never begin to live fully until one comes to terms with the inevitability of one's own death. But it is much easier to say than to accomplish. The task that confronts us is how to remain positive, productive and peaceful in the face of the inevitable. This is my strategy.

> I say to myself,
> "I AM GOING TO DIE.
> WE ARE ALL GOING TO DIE.
> WHEN? NO ONE KNOWS.
> IS THERE ANYTHING I CAN DO TO CHANGE THIS?
> NO."

SO I DON'T WASTE TIME WORRYING ABOUT SOMETHING OVER WHICH I HAVE NO CONTROL.

When anxiety and fear come, as they do, I dismiss them and replace them with some of the following hope-filled thoughts. They help me a lot and I hope they do the same for you.

"I want to tell you I have absolutely no doubt now that there is a transformation of consciousness at the point of death and we go on."
    Dr. Raymond Moody

"The Blazing evidence of immortality is our dissatisfaction with any other solution."
    Emerson

"Until we love completely all things can hurt us."
    Thomas Merton

"There is no path so dark
  nor road so steep
  nor hill so slippery
  that other people have not been there before me
  and survived."
    M. Bedrosian

The tide of eternity sweeps in and life and death are two halves of the one whole. One day we shall understand the mystery, but not yet. Now we journey with faith, remembering that God said, " Let there be light."
    Gladys Taber

"She has out-soared the shadow of our night."
    Shelly

Grief is the price we pay for having loved deeply. A difficult price to be sure, but one we willingly pay for the joy of loving.

"I am fully persuaded and assured that death is very much like birth. It is the traumatic but essential passage into a new phase of life. It will so far surpass anything we have ever dreamed of as to make all present attempts to describe it seem tawdry and utterly inept."
Tom Harpur

"Another speculation of mine is that we enjoy ourselves hereafter by having what we called happiness on earth repeated in a finer tone and so repeated."
Keats

I picked up a copy of one of the seniors' publications that seem to be everywhere these days. On reading it I noticed articles and ads on the following: pre-need funeral planning, hearing aids, dentures, the Casket Store, memorial tree planting, monuments, nursing homes, getting your financial house in order and my favourite, LEAKAGE.

I think I would like to focus on new adventures, and new exciting possibilities. When I start to leak I might change my mind. Until then, thanks anyway.

It was a beautiful summer day as my 78 year old father and I sat overlooking Lake Huron enjoying a wee drink before dinner. In the course of our conversation I asked him if he minded being old. He looked at me with a twinkle in his eye and said, "Not when you consider the alternative."

LIFE AND ETERNITY

*If I should never see the moon again
Rising red gold across the harvest field,
Or feel the stinging of soft April rain
As the brown earth her hidden treasures yield.*

*If I should never taste the salt sea spray
As the ship beats her course against the breeze,
Or smell the dog rose and the new mown hay
Or moss and primrose beneath the tree.*

*If I should never hear the thrushes wake
Long before sunrise in the glimmering dawn,
Or watch the huge Atlantic rollers break
Against the rugged cliffs in baffling scorn.*

*If I have said goodbye to stream and wood
To the wide ocean and the green clad hill,
I know that God who made this world so good
Has somewhere made a heaven better still.*

*This I bear witness with my latest breath,
Knowing God I fear not death.*

This poem was found in the bible of
Major Malcolm Boyle who
was killed in action on D-Day 1944.

"JUST WHERE IS THIS HILL YOU KEEP SAYING DAD IS OVER?"

MY SUMMER OF SADNESS

When I turned fifty I experienced an entire summer of sadness. It wasn't serious depression for I slept well, ate well, and felt no serious lethargy. I just felt sad for about two months.

Looking back I realize that my blues resulted from a series of life situations I was confronting at the time. My parents were approaching eighty, with the strong sense of closure that age implies. Our youngest son was preparing to enter university that fall and letting go was going to be difficult.

When I went for my medical my doctor, who was a mere youngster in his early thirties, remarked that I had a good twenty years ahead of me, leaving me to face the stark reality that I had more sidewalk behind me than ahead of me. If the next twenty years went by as quickly as the last I would be entering eternity in no time.

This kind of thinking was definitely eroding my usual sense of joy. I couldn't let it continue, especially when I spend much of my time sharing the joy and the wonder of being alive with people everywhere.

It didn't take long after re-reading the inspirational literature that had formed me and following the advice I give to others for the cloud to lift allowing me to return to joy.

PARENTING/ FAMILY

If raising children was meant to be easy it wouldn't begin with something called labour.

Have you ever considered the possibility that grandparents and grandchildren get along so well because they share a common enemy?

My mother started jogging at the age of 60. She is now 83 and nobody knows where the hell she is.

The grade one teacher wrote a note to the parents of one of her students expressing concern that the young man had no friends among his fellow students. The parents were quite concerned because they had never noticed the problem at home and in their neighbourhood. When they asked their son why he had such a hard time making friends at school he replied that they had told him not to play with anyone who used bad language in the playground.

If you don't want your kids to hear what you're saying, pretend that you're talking to them.

WHEN THEY WERE KIDS THEY WERE SO CUTE I COULD HAVE EATEN THEM. NOW THAT THEY'RE TEENS I WISH I HAD.
M.M.

The three most dreaded words by fathers everywhere:
"SOME ASSEMBLY REQUIRED"

My wife was on the phone obviously speaking to someone she hadn't heard from for a long time. As I passed by I casually asked, "Who's on the phone?" To which she replied, "I am."

Before my teenage daughter left for one of her frequent sleepovers I said what any parent would say on such an occasion, "Make sure you get a good night's sleep." She looked at me with unbelieving eyes and said, "Dad, everybody knows that you don't sleep at a sleep-over." Silly me!

The best substitute for experience is being sixteen years old.

I have concluded that there are five M's in the life of every teenage girl: MEN, MALLS, MAKE-UP, MUSIC and MOVIES. Certainly doesn't leave much time for DAD.

Have you ever wondered how a child who is afraid of the dark quickly becomes a teenager who wants to say out all night?

Sometimes we give teenagers credit for knowing more than they actually do. This became apparent to me in my Family Life class when a bright, attractive seventeen year old female student stood to give her opinion on birth control. She looked directly at me and said, "Sir, I think it is a good idea for a woman to have a vasectomy if she feels that she doesn't want to have any more children." By the way, many of the other students sat nodding their heads in agreement.

Why is it that just when you have the shape for the job, your kids stop believing in Santa Claus?

A friend recently suggested to me that every first born child enters this world with one enormous responsibility: to teach the mother and father how to parent. Shouldn't there be a manual?

"A FATHER TELLING HIS SON TO DO HIS HOMEWORK DOES NOT CONSTITUTE CHILD ABUSE."

I always recommend that parents take their teenagers camping one at a time. There is something about sitting under a star-studded sky around a campfire that loosens the otherwise tight teenage tongue. Revelation after revelation pour forth if you only sit quietly and just say, "Oh, really."

Be prepared to hear things you would rather not hear and be prepared to resist the overwhelming urge to preach, moralize and pontificate. GOOD LUCK!

When alone, one on one with your teenager, you aren't distracted by the competitive interplay that exists when your children are together. You also won't have to worry about being relegated to the sidelines while they laugh and joke with one another concerning things about which you know absolutely nothing in a language you can't quite understand.

NO MATTER THE TROUBLE
THEY GIVE YOU,
NO MATTER THE PAIN AND THE SORROW,

ALWAYS,
ALWAYS REMEMBER...
YOU'LL BE LAUGHING ABOUT THIS
TOMORROW!

HEALING THE EARTH

One can't write about human well being without commenting on the state of our environment, for our well being as individuals and as a species is contingent upon a healthy planet.

The three fundamental prerequisites for human well being are clean air to breathe, uncontaminated food to eat and pure water to drink. All other human needs mean very little if these fundamentals are not realized. Maslow suggests that only when the basic needs are satisfied will we invest time and energy in meeting the others. Yet we seem determined to
decimate the very planet that sustains us in the interest of profit and greed.

There is no question, nature will survive our abuse. The only question is whether we, as a species, will survive as a part of nature.

The following story illustrates the type of thinking that has resulted in the continued destruction of our earth, thinking that must change if we are to heal our wounded planet and survive. A construction crew was in the process of preparing valuable land for another strip mall. (Just what every community in North America needs, another mall.) When a decision had to be made as to which of the numerous mature trees should be cut down the crew boss was heard to say, "Cut them all down. They shouldn't be growing here anyway." I guess it is true that our society has been built on the belief that if it grows, cut it down; if it moves, shoot it.

EITHER/OR

I read recently about a politician saying that if there is a choice to be made between the quality of the air we breathe and putting bread on the table, air quality will come in second. Why does it have to be an either/or issue? Somehow barbequed steak doesn't sound so appealing if I can't breathe while eating it.

WHO'S PROBLEM?

Each summer we hear about the Canada Goose problem experienced by many communities throughout Canada. Goose droppings are contaminating beaches and private property. Flocks are increasing and no one seems to have a solution acceptable to all.

Why is it that humans always have the problem with animals? In my mind it's the animals that have the much greater problem with people. We have contaminated their water often resulting in genetic mutations in their young. Their habitat is consumed by our voracious appetite for development in the name of progress. Their air and nesting sites are polluted by chemical spills and garbage of all kinds.

We feed them to keep them around for our amusement and when they do what nature compels them to do on our lawns and beaches we suddenly develop a goose problem.
WHO HAS THE PROBLEM?

WISDOM AND NATURE

I have always had a love affair with the natural world. Being born and raised in Northern Ontario provided me with everything I needed to satisfy my passion.

Sault Ste. Marie is located on the St. Mary's River separating Lake Superior from Lake Huron. It is a world of rocky hills, pine trees, beautiful lakes and rivers and sunsets to die for. It was here that my love affair blossomed. Even though my work has taken me from the north, the north has never been taken from me. Each summer I return drawn by some powerful magnetic force to be saturated with its beauty and formed by its solitude. It is in this awesome solitude that I reflect on the meaning of life, contemplate the mysteries of the universe and celebrate the sheer joy of being alive. I would like to share with you a few of my reflections. I hope you enjoy reading them as much as I enjoyed experiencing them.

Look to the heavens on a star-studded night. Embrace the awesome beauty of the universe and let it embrace and comfort you in return.

I love to sit in solitude beside the water and watch the undulating rhythm of the waves as they pound or caress the shore. Knowing that this process has gone on undisturbed for thousands of years gives me an overwhelming sense of the eternal reach of time.

This line from Gibran never ceases to console me, "The sea never sleeps, and in its vigil there is consolation for the troubled soul."

If there is no God then the stars are a staircase to nowhere.

One of my favourite writers is Pierre Teilhard de Chardin, a poet, scientist and theologian who wrote prolifically about the evolving nature of the material and spiritual world and our place in them. This is one of my best loved quotations:

"TO UNDERSTAND THE WORLD
KNOWLEDGE IS NOT ENOUGH,
YOU HAVE TO SEE IT,
TOUCH IT,
LIVE IN ITS PRESENCE,
AND DRINK THE VITAL HEAT OF
EXISTENCE
AT THE VERY HEART OF REALITY."

When I was a teenager I used to go to a place called Gros Cap just west of Sault Ste. Marie where Lake Superior enters the St. Mary's River. There I would sit on a hill overlooking the lake to watch the sunset. Life was good, so good that I recall never wanting it to end. It wasn't until much later that I came upon a quotation from Pierre Teilhard de Chardin that spoke to me about the eternal dimension of life and the universe. "Mankind has every right to be anxious about their fate so long as we feel ourselves to be lost and lonely in the midst of the mass of created things. But let us once discover that our fate is bound up with the fate of nature itself and immediately, joyously, we will begin again our forward march."

This belief that everything I enjoy and embrace within the natural world will somehow be part of eternity eliminates the sense of cosmic grief I experienced as a young man at the thought of having the beauty of the material world end when heaven began. I now see the material universe as an integral part of eternity and not as something we shed or discard after our time here is over.

> "To be alone, out of doors on a still, soft, clear, moonlit night is, to me, one of the greatest pleasures this world can give."
> Francis Kilvert

> "I can enjoy society in a room, but out of doors nature is enough company for me. I am never less alone than when I am alone in nature."
> William Hazlitt

> "Listen to the voice of the wind, and the ceaseless message that forms itself out of the silence."
> Rainer Marie Rilke

RANDOM REFLECTIONS

I have concluded that middle age for men is that time of life when you have more hair growing from your ears and your nose than on your head.

———————————

Why is it that when you're feeling great you stop doing the things you did faithfully to help you feel that way?

———————————

Many people say to me that they have no time to read, but if everyone read every time they went to the bathroom can you imagine the number of books they could go through in a lifetime? (A moving thought, don't you think?)

———————————

No one can motivate anyone to do anything. You can only provide incentives for them to motivate themselves.

———————————

Perhaps today is called the present because it is a gift to cherish.

———————————

Whoever said, "Everyone wants to live a long time, but no one wants to get old," was right on target.

We are truly fortunate if we have one person in our life who cares enough to listen to us. With such good fortune comes the responsibility to care enough to listen in return.

I think it was Mark Twain who said, "A bore is someone who wants to talk about himself or herself when I want to talk about myself."

There is nothing more flattering or rare than the undivided attention of another.

Very few people are good conversationalists. Sitting around in a group can soon become tedious if you are the only one asking questions and listening to answers. At some point it must become reciprocal to be conversation. We seem to be preoccupied with our own agenda to the exclusion of another's.

We live in a world of instant gratification. "I want what I want when I want it." Waiting has become a lost art.

A wise man once said to me, "Mike I can't give you the secret to success, but I can share the secret to failure. Try to please everyone." Even knowing this to be true we continue to try.

The negative draws attention to itself; the positive often goes unnoticed. I can give a talk that is well received and enjoyed by the majority of the audience. But let one or two evaluations come back with negative comments and what do I focus on? You guessed it, the negative.

I remember my daughter, Beth, laughing quietly with a friend in church prior to the service and evoking the wrath of two very devout people in front of us. They turned with scowls on their faces as if the girls had just committed the ultimate sin. I guess it is O.K. to make a joyful noise unto the Lord as long as you don't do it in church.

I once met the mother of a former student of mine and asked her how her son was. She proceeded to tell me that he was making a six figure income, had thirty six people under him, a home in the suburbs with a tennis court and an
in-ground pool. I never did find out how he was.

Brian Tracey, in his book, "Maximum Achievement" said that everything we do in life is motivated by either a search for love or by the response to love's absence from our lives. There is something about this that certainly rings true when you think about it.

I was in one of the huge department stores around Christmas when I saw a father with his very young son walk by a picture of Santa Claus smoking a pipe. He looked at the smoking Santa and said, "How can smoking be such a bad thing when the nicest man in the world smokes a pipe?" I could not believe my ears.

I saw this item on one of the many reality programs on television. A woman on death row was being interviewed a week or so before her execution. Apparently she had killed her husband, her disabled child and her lover. When the interviewer asked her how she wanted to be remembered she thought for a moment and then replied, "I want to be remembered as a good mother."

I drive the speed limit, or slightly above, in spite of the fact that everyone else on the highway drives 20 or 30 km over it. In my family, therefore, I have the reputation for being a slowpoke.

My mother, who lives in a home on the North Channel of Lake Huron outside the town of Thessalon Ontario, had invited our niece and nephew to visit her and enjoy the wonder and beauty of Algoma District. Carol and I, with Beth our teenaged daughter started out a day ahead. Pat and Frank would leave the next day.

The trip is about 700 km., well within one day's drive. Pat and Frank were driving along west of Sudbury when they saw a van like mine. Frank remarked, "That looks like Mike ahead." To which Pat replied, "It could be, he did leave yesterday." I'm so happy to be able to provide therapeutic humour for the members of my family.

Have you ever noticed how the word, "BUT" can be used as a very effective erasure of any good that preceded it? "You did a great job, BUT...." There goes your great job!

It never fails. Whenever I have been with people I like and enjoy I find it difficult to say goodbye. I know for certain that when we part company I will be sad for two days. A friend once told me, on parting, that in heaven there are no goodbyes. I hope she's right.

Some people think their lives are full when really they are just cluttered.

A very dear friend of ours is living with cancer of the pancreas. She has a wonderful sense of humour which I'm sure is helping her wage her tenacious battle against this terrible disease. Recently we had a party in her honour to give support and show her that she's loved and not alone in her struggle. As she sat with us I was struck by the positive atmosphere that existed in the midst of obvious pain and suffering. Within great sadness there was joy and within great joy there was sadness.

JUST FOR THE FUN OF IT!

A BORE IS ALWAYS "ME" DEEP IN CONVERSATION.

REMEMBER WHEN THAT STILL SMALL VOICE WAS YOUR CONSCIENCE?
NOW IT'S YOUR IPOD.

ANYONE WHO SAYS SWIMMING IS GOOD FOR THE FIGURE HAS NEVER REALLY TAKEN A GOOD LOOK AT A WHALE!

ALWAYS BORROW MONEY FROM A PESSIMIST... THEY DON'T EXPECT TO BE PAID BACK!

HEAR NO EVIL...
SEE NO EVIL...
SPEAK NO EVIL...
AND NO ONE WILL WANT TO TALK TO YOU!

"WHAT YOU WANT FOR YOUR ALLERGIES IS ALLEGRA, NOT VIAGRA."

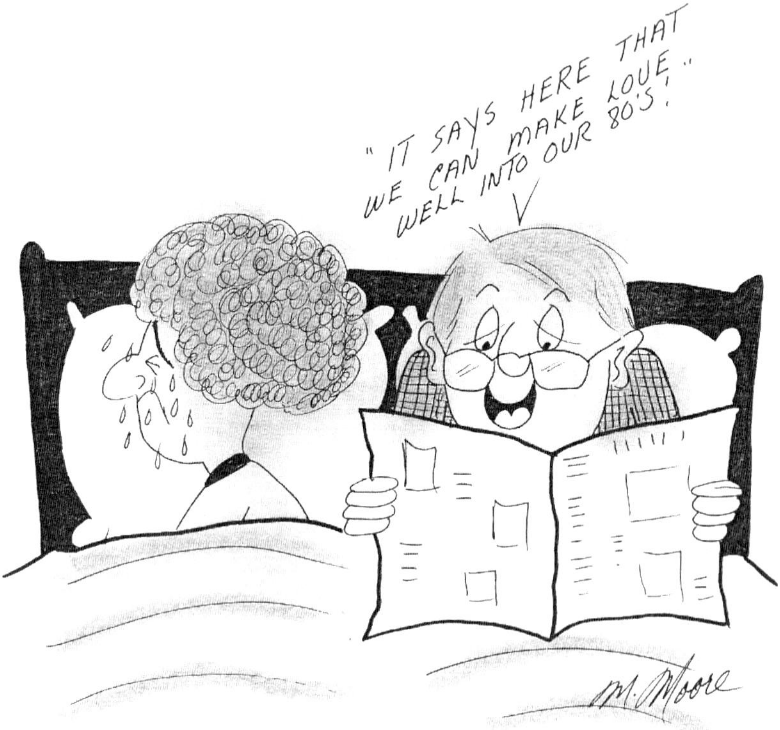
"IT SAYS HERE THAT WE CAN MAKE LOVE WELL INTO OUR 80'S!"
M. Moore

GLOBAL WARMING MY FOOT!

THERE'S NOTHING LIKE A FISHING TRIP TO MAKE RETIREMENT WHAT IT SHOULD BE! RIGHT HONEY?
M. Moore

"OK, SO YOU DON'T HAVE LOVE HANDLES.....JUST A ROLL OF FAT HANGING OVER YOUR BELT."

EPILOGUE

I am under no illusion that the words of one person can change the world in any significant way, but I do believe that when two people meet between the covers of a book insights can be shared which can have a profound impact on lives everywhere.

When Gladys Taber (who is quoted in the section on aging and death) died, I actually felt that I had lost a dear friend even though I had never met her except through the pages of her books. Her attitude toward life, death and the rhythms and joys of the natural world enriched my own existence beyond measure. Such is the power of the printed word.

It is my hope that in, "Embracing the Mystery" you were able to find the elements of joy, wonder and awe in abundance as we stand in the presence of Mystery. A mystery which engulfs us, affirms us, comforts us, and gives us hope that what we know and love in creation will never end.

LET THE MYSTERY UNFOLD AND THE LAUGHTER CONTINUE.

The greatest gifts we can give one another are the gifts of time, attention and laughter.

Thank you
Mike Moore